WITHDRAWN

Peyton Manning

Champion Football Star

MANNING

18

Enslow Publishers, Inc.
40 Industrial Road
Box 398
Berkeley Heights, NJ 07922
USA

http://www.enslow.com

Ken Rappoport

Original edition published as *Super Sports Star Peyton Manning* in 2003.

Library of Congress Cataloging-in-Publication Data

Rappoport, Ken.
  Peyton Manning : champion football star / Ken Rappoport.
    p. cm. — (Sports star champions)
  Includes index.
  Summary: "Explores the life and career of quarterback Peyton Manning, including his high school and college career, his rise to stardom in the NFL, and his remarkable achievements with the Indianapolis Colts"—Provided by publisher.
  ISBN 978-0-7660-4027-4
  1. Manning, Peyton—Juvenile literature. 2. Football players—United States—Biography—Juvenile literature. 3. Quarterbacks (Football)—United States—Biography—Juvenile literature. I. Title.
  GV939.M289R368 2013
  796.332092—dc23
  [B]
                2011052759

Future editions:
Paperback ISBN 978-1-4644-0162-6
ePUB ISBN 978-1-4645-1069-4
PDF ISBN 978-1-4646-1069-1

Printed in the United States of America

032012 Lake Book Manufacturing, Inc., Melrose Park, IL

10 9 8 7 6 5 4 3 2 1

J-B
MANNING
423-6413

To Our Readers: We have done our best to make sure all Internet addresses in this book were active and appropriate when we went to press. However, the author and the publisher have no control over and assume no liability for the material available on those Internet sites or on other Web sites they may link to. Any comments or suggestions can be sent by e-mail to comments@enslow.com or to the address on the back cover.

♻ Enslow Publishers, Inc., is committed to printing our books on recycled paper. The paper in every book contains 10% to 30% post-consumer waste (PCW). The cover board on the outside of each book contains 100% PCW. Our goal is to do our part to help young people and the environment too!

Illustration Credits: AP Images / Alan Diaz, p. 27; AP Images / Amy Sancetta, pp. 6, 11, 39; AP Images / Bill Baptist, p. 12; AP Images / Chris O'Meara, p. 36; AP Images / Darron Cummings, p. 9; AP Images / David Drapkin, p. 4; AP Images / David Duprey, p. 41; AP Images / David Stluka, pp. 30, 42; AP Images / David Zalubowski, pp. 1, 44 AP Images / Ed Reinke, p. 21; AP Images / Greg Trott, p. 24; AP Images / Marco Garcia, p. 34; AP Images / Mark Humphrey, pp. 18, 22; AP Images / Matt Stamey, p. 16; AP Images / Michael Conroy, pp. 14, 32; AP Images / Ronen Zilberman, p. 5; AP Images / Steve Nesius, p. 28.

Cover Illustration: AP Images / David Zalubowski (Peyton Manning holds up his new Denver Broncos' jersey at a press conference announcing his signing with the team on March 20, 2012).

Contents

Introduction

Denver Broncos' superstar Peyton Manning could be the perfect quarterback for today's game. He is six feet five inches tall and weighs 230 pounds. He is strong and has one of the quickest releases in football. It is the reason that Manning usually is difficult to bring down and has very few of his passes intercepted.

Manning is one of the most accurate passers in football history. He is especially good at running the two-minute drill, leading his team down the field when steel nerves are required at the end of a game. Few are more prepared than Manning.

Sports Illustrated called Manning "the league's hardest working QB."

Peyton Manning's brilliant skills made the Indianapolis Colts one of the best teams in the NFL during his career there.

But that is not the only reason he is considered an all-time great quarterback. Manning is a "thinking man's" quarterback. He is able to change plays at the line of scrimmage on the fly, which he often does. Few quarterbacks are given as much freedom to call plays on their own like Manning.

Manning learned to love the game when he was a kid. His father, Archie Manning, was also a star quarterback. He played for the New Orleans Saints. Peyton learned from his dad what it takes to be a leader and a winner. Manning never stops practicing. He is always working hard to make himself better.

No wonder Manning became a top quarterback in the National Football League (NFL) in a very short time and is headed for the Hall of Fame.

Peyton Manning followed his father's footsteps in becoming a great NFL quarterback.

Peyton Manning throws a pass against the New England Patriots in the third quarter of the AFC Championship game on January 21, 2007. Trailing at halftime, 21–6, the Colts needed a superstar performance from their quarterback in the second half to mount a comeback.

Battle of the Quarterbacks

It was the 2007 American Football Conference (AFC) Championship game. It was one last chance for Peyton Manning before another knockout in the playoffs.

It had all been so familiar: Since joining the Indianapolis Colts in 1998, the star quarterback had put together incredible offensive numbers and won many individual awards. One accomplishment was missing: He had not won a Super Bowl, as had been expected of the NFL's most-talented and hardest-working quarterback. Eight seasons, eight times shut out from the NFL's championship game.

Now trailing the arch-rival New England Patriots, 21–6, at halftime of their AFC title game, it looked like it was going to be another playoff loss for the Colts.

The Patriots had already humbled the Colts in two prior postseason games and won three of the previous five Super Bowls behind their own quarterbacking great, Tom Brady. The two quarterbacks were constantly being compared as the NFL's best. Manning's critics pointed out the obvious: Brady had won three Super Bowls; Manning had yet to win his first.

The Colts-Patriots rivalry had become one of the most competitive in the NFL, particularly after New England dominated Manning in the 2003 AFC title game. Manning had won his first Most Valuable Player award during that season. It was an award he would win many times over. But he didn't look anything like an MVP in the playoffs against the Patriots. With the top-ranked defense in the league, New England intercepted Manning four times and sacked him another four times in a 24–14 Patriots victory.

As one of the top quarterbacks in football and the Colts' acknowledged team leader, Manning had taken a lot of the criticism for the Colts' playoff failures.

A great quarterback, yes, but he can't win the big game. That's what the critics said about Manning.

The locker room at the Colts' RCA Dome in the 2007 AFC title game was like a tomb at halftime, the players preparing for what could be the end of the season for them. No one was more crushed than Manning, especially after one of his passes was intercepted and returned for a Patriots touchdown in the second quarter.

Time for a pep talk from Colts head coach Tony Dungy.

"I'm telling you, this is our game," Dungy said as he walked among the players. "It's our time."

If anyone else had said that, it would sound corny. Not from Dungy, however.

Peyton Manning gestures and calls out a play at the line of scrimmage during the AFC Championship game. Manning had struggled in previous playoff contests against the Patriots, but the star quarterback would not let his team down in this game.

"He has a way of making you believe," Manning said.

Dungy reminded his players of the 2003 game during the regular season. The Colts had trailed the Patriots, 31–10, before making a great comeback to fall just a yard short. The Colts lost, 38–34.

"This gap is easier to close," Dungy told his team at his halftime talk. "We get the ball first, and if we score a touchdown on our first drive, we're only one score down."

The encouraged Manning came out firing in the second half. He drove the Colts 76 yards on a 14-play drive.

Then after the Pats went three and out, Manning took the Colts on another touchdown drive, this time finishing it with a pass for a two-point conversion.

Game tied, 21–21.

Both quarterbacks went into high gear, filling the air with footballs. The teams went back and forth trading the lead. It was a battle between the NFL's two greatest quarterbacks of their era, both on their way to the Hall of Fame.

With 2:17 to go in the game, Manning's Colts trailed, 34–31, when the All-Pro quarterback trotted onto the field.

First down, 80 yards to go.

Could Manning do it? Could he finally break the hated Patriots' curse?

Connecting on one pass after another, Manning worked quickly with his patented two-minute drill. Suddenly, the Colts were on the Patriots' 11-yard line as precious seconds ticked off the clock.

Manning then sent running back Joseph Addai into the middle of the line. Addai scraped and battled for the needed yards.

Touchdown!

The 38–34 victory sent the Colts to their first Super Bowl berth in thirty-six years. Their opponents: the Chicago Bears.

Could anything stop them from finally winning the Super Bowl now?

Peyton Manning grew up around professional football players. His father, Archie Manning, was a star quarterback for the New Orleans Saints. Young Peyton ran around on the stadium fields after games dreaming of one day playing in the NFL.

Born to Be a Quarterback

Imagine if you could see an NFL game from the sidelines. You could go into the locker room after the game. You could talk to your favorite stars. You could be on the field playing catch. Not in your backyard, but in an actual NFL stadium. Growing up, Peyton Manning was able to do just that.

Petyon's father was a famous quarterback. Archie Manning was named a college All-American at the University of Mississippi. He was an All-Pro with the New Orleans Saints.

Being the son of Archie Manning had its rewards. Sundays were spent in the New Orleans Superdome watching his father play. When the game was over, the fans

Peyton Manning drops back to pass during practice at the Indianapolis Colts' training camp in Terre Haute, Indiana. Even as a kid, Peyton had a great work ethic and loved to practice. He studied his father's game films to learn more about playing quarterback.

went home. Peyton did not go home. He went to the locker room with his older brother, Cooper. They ate candy bars and made footballs out of tape. Out on the NFL field, they played football. Peyton wanted to be a football star just like his dad.

Peyton Manning was born on March 24, 1976. He grew up in the city of New Orleans, Louisiana. In a big yellow house, he would lie awake at night and listen to tapes of old radio broadcasts of his father's games. Peyton loved to hear stories about his father's college days.

Peyton loved football. His older brother, Cooper, and younger brother, Eli, loved the sport, too.

In the eighth grade, Peyton started thinking about a football career. "I started working at the (quarterback) position a little bit," Peyton said. "I'd ask questions of my dad and my teammates." Peyton was a hard worker. He spent a lot of his time studying his father's game films. He knew more about football than almost anyone his age.

Peyton was only in his second year of high school when he was named the starting quarterback. He played for Isidore Newman, a small private school. And guess who was Peyton's favorite receiver? His brother Cooper—the school's star pass catcher.

From left to right, Cooper, Archie, Peyton, and Eli Manning pose for a photo at the Manning Passing Academy in Thibodaux, Louisiana. The Manning brothers all played football growing up in Louisiana. In high school, Peyton, the star quarterback, threw passes to his brother Cooper, the star receiver at Isidore Newman High School.

Peyton had an amazing high school career. He passed for more than 7,000 yards. He also had 92 touchdown passes. He led his school to thirty-four wins. He only lost five games in three seasons. Stories about Peyton were in national sports magazines and newspapers. He was also on television.

All the nation's top college football programs wanted Peyton to play for them. But which school would Peyton Manning choose?

Peyton Manning races toward the end zone to score a touchdown against the Georgia Bulldogs on September 9, 1995. Manning made an immediate impact on the Volunteers, helping the team win six of seven games when he started at quarterback.

Bowling Them Over

It was college decision day. In a room filled with reporters and television cameras, Peyton Manning stepped to the microphone. Then he surprised the sports world.

It had been a tough choice for Manning. His father had starred at the University of Mississippi. His brother Cooper had played there before an injury ended his career. Manning was expected to go there, too. Instead, he chose the University of Tennessee. He thought he had a better chance of winning there.

"I wanted to follow my heart," Manning said at the 1994 news conference. "But instead I followed my mind."

The decision created a lot of bad feelings. He received letters from angry Mississippi fans.

Manning thought he was going to spend his first year watching from the sidelines. In the season's fourth game against Mississippi State, the Tennessee Volunteers' starting quarterback was hurt. The back-up quarterback was also injured. Now Manning had to carry the team. He had to become a leader. It was scary: He was only a freshman in his first month of college football.

The game was tied, 7–7, just before halftime. The ball was on the Tennessee 22-yard line. It was a long way—78 yards—to the goal line. Play after play, Manning moved the Volunteers down the field. The Volunteers moved the ball inside the 20-yard line when Manning found a receiver open in the end zone. He fired a pass. Touchdown! The Volunteers led, 14–7.

Even though the Volunteers lost that game, Manning showed he was a leader.

Manning was back in the lineup the following week. And the Volunteers started winning. With Manning as a starter, they won six of seven games. He had helped turn a losing team into a winning one.

"Peyton's becoming a very confident quarterback," said guard Kevin Mayes. "There's a different look in his eye now when he steps into a huddle."

It was hard to believe that Manning, only in his first year at college, was leading his team to the Gator Bowl. Starting in his first bowl game, Manning led the Vols to victory over the Virginia Tech Hokies.

Although Manning was younger than most of the other players on the field, he had lifted his team to great heights. He was confident. He was growing up quickly in the fast-paced world of big-time college football.

Peyton Manning looks for an open receiver as a defender chases him during the second quarter of a game against Kentucky. The Tennessee quarterback led the Volunteers to two consecutive Citrus Bowl victories.

In his second season, Manning led Tennessee to nine straight victories. The Volunteers capped the year with a 20–14 win over Ohio State in the Citrus Bowl. It was an amazing season for Peyton Manning. He set a college record when only four of his 380 passes were intercepted.

The next season, Manning led the Volunteers back to the Citrus Bowl. This time, they beat Northwestern, 48–28.

Peyton Manning takes the field for his last Volunteers' home game on November 29, 1997, in Knoxville, Tennessee. In his final season, Manning broke several collegiate records.

Manning was also working hard in the classroom. After three years, he had enough credits to graduate with honors. He could leave school one year early to join the NFL.

He made his decision: He would stay in school for his senior year.

Manning's decision to stay in school surprised some people. Many star athletes leave school early to go to the pros. They want to move on. But college football was too much fun for Manning. He did not want to give it up just yet. As he said, "I came back to create more memories."

Manning wanted to make his final year in college a special one. And he did. He led the Volunteers to win after win. Manning's play had caught the attention of the nation. By the time he graduated, he had broken thirty-three school records. He also broke several national records. He led the Volunteers to an outstanding 39–6 record as a starter.

Manning had been number one in the hearts of Tennessee fans. Then he was selected number one in the NFL draft. The Indianapolis Colts made Peyton Manning the top pick. Manning was proud of the honor. However, he knew he still had to prove himself as a pro. "I'm looking forward to the challenge," he said.

Peyton Manning surveys the field as he looks for an open receiver during a game against the San Francisco 49ers in his rookie season with the Colts.

CHAPTER
FOUR

A Frisky Colt

Peyton Manning was struggling. Four games into the 1998 NFL season, he was still looking for his first victory. The Colts finished with a woeful 3–13 record. In one season in the pros, Peyton Manning had lost two more games than in his eight years of high school and college ball combined.

But there was also some good news. Manning had put together the best rookie season in NFL history. He was the only NFL quarterback to have taken every snap for his team in 1998. With twenty-six touchdown passes, he broke Charlie Conerly's rookie record. That was a big deal in

the Manning household, because Conerly was an All-Star quarterback at Mississippi and the New York Giants in the NFL. The Mannings all loved him. "I'm not a big individual records guy," Manning said, "but that's kind of special."

Now all Peyton had to do was learn how to win in the pros. It didn't seem possible to go from last to first in one season. But Manning and his teammates were doing their best to make it happen.

It was only Manning's second year in the NFL. Yet he was the best-known player on his team. The Colts had one of the NFL's top offenses in 1999. The Colts' defense was also strong.

Manning's football work habits had not changed since he was eleven years old. "He's always working on something," said Colts defensive end Mark Thomas. "He's here [practice field] early and stays late."

When Manning's practice was over, he did extra work on his own. He joined the special teams practice. He ran up and down the field on kickoff coverage. And then he did more passing practice. Finally, he studied videotapes and the playbook.

The victories piled up. The Colts had completely reversed their poor 3–13 record in 1998 with a 13–3 record in 1999.

Although Peyton Manning had a solid rookie season, the Colts struggled to a 3–13 record. However, just one year later, Manning and the Colts improved dramatically, winning ten more games. In this photo, Manning drops back to pass against the Miami Dolphins on December 5, 1999.

Peyton Manning throws a pass against the Tampa Bay Buccaneers during the Colts' dramatic fourth-quarter rally on October 6, 2003. Known for his late-game heroics, Manning overcame a 21-point deficit in the final five minutes to lead the Colts to victory.

The Colts were going to the playoffs. It was the greatest turnaround in NFL history.

Suddenly, the Colts had become one of the NFL's top teams. Manning staked his claim as one of the league's best young quarterbacks. Hardly a season went by that Manning wasn't named to the All-Pro team. In 2003, Manning won the first of his numerous Most Valuable Player awards.

One game that emphasized his amazing talents occurred in 2003, an appearance on Monday Night Football against the defending Super Bowl champion Tampa Bay Buccaneers.

Manning and the Colts looked hopelessly out of contention, trailing Tampa Bay, 35–14, in the final five minutes.

Manning led the Colts to a quick touchdown. The Colts then recovered an onside kick. On fourth down with six yards to go, Manning hooked up with Marvin Harrison on a 28-yard touchdown pass. That cut the Buccaneers' lead to just 35–28.

Only 1:41 to go. Manning drove the Colts 85 yards down the field for the game-tying touchdown.

The teams went into overtime. Manning set up a 29-yard field goal for the winning points. The Colts had pulled out an amazing 38–35 victory. It was only a hint of things to come for the great quarterback.

Peyton Manning fires a pass downfield during a 41–10 victory against the Chicago Bears on November 21, 2004. Manning built on an already successful career with a record-breaking season in 2004.

Super Season

Look out, Dan Marino! Peyton Manning is about to make football history.

"It has been a fun ride this year," Manning said in the 2004 season.

No quarterback in league history had been as consistent. Manning became the only player in history to throw for 4,000 yards or more in six consecutive seasons.

The most fun for Manning was chasing after Marino's single-season record of 48 touchdown passes. Manning loved being compared to Marino and other Hall of Fame greats.

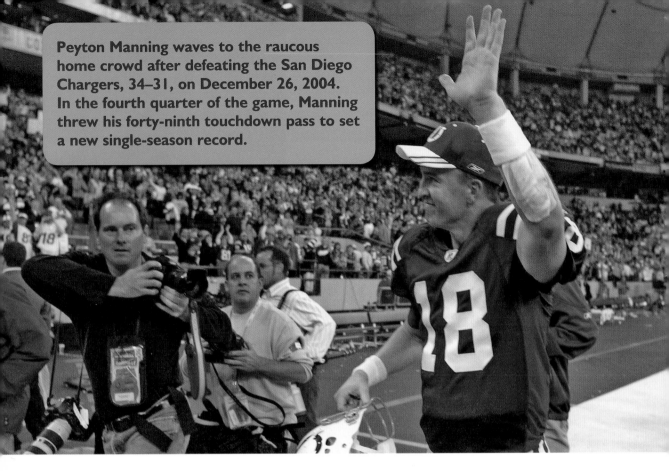

"Just being with those names makes it more special," Manning said. "I am very humbled to be on that list."

In December 2004, Manning faced the San Diego Chargers. One more touchdown pass to tie Marino's record, two to break it.

But it seemed everything was going wrong for Manning. He had missed three good chances to complete a touchdown pass: A first-quarter pass was intercepted near the goal line; another pass was broken up at the 3-yard line; one more pass glanced off a receiver's hands in the end zone.

Finally, in the third quarter, Manning shoveled a 3-yard touchdown pass to James Mungro. Number 48 was in the books.

One more touchdown pass to break Marino's record.

A buzz went through the crowd. The fans were excited about Manning's chase for the record. Manning had to be at his best. The Colts were trying to play catch-up. They trailed the Chargers by 15 points in the fourth quarter.

Manning drove the Colts downfield for a score. Then, with 56 seconds left in regulation, Manning fired a 21-yard touchdown pass to Brandon Stokley for the record breaker. More importantly, the Colts had tied the game and sent it into overtime. Manning set up a field goal to give the Colts a dramatic 34–31 victory.

Up Close

In 2004, Manning broke an NFL record by throwing at least two touchdown passes in thirteen straight games. He had shared the record with Brett Favre, who set the original mark with the Green Bay Packers.

It was the highlight of a season of highlights for Manning. He was just about everyone's player of the year after throwing 49 touchdown passes and a career-high 4,557 yards. Other awesome stats: a 67.6 percent completion mark and a record passer rating of 121.1.

Peyton and Eli Manning stand on the field together at the end of the NFL Pro Bowl game in Honolulu, Hawaii, on February 8, 2009. The first time the two brothers played against each other in the NFL, Peyton's Colts defeated Eli's New York Giants, 26–21.

"He's the conductor of our train and he's got our train really rolling," said Colts coach Tony Dungy after Manning led the Colts to another playoff appearance.

In 2006, the Colts won their first nine games behind Manning. That included a 26–21 victory over brother Eli's New York Giants team (in the first "Manning Bowl").

In the Wild Card playoff game, the Colts whipped the Kansas City Chiefs, 23–8, as Manning connected on 30 of 38 passes.

The Colts faced a tougher opponent the following week, the Baltimore Ravens. The Colts led, 12–6, with 7:39 to go in the fourth quarter. Manning's job was to eat up the clock so that the Ravens could not get back on the field for a late rally, as they were known to do. Manning did his job. The Colts escaped with a tight victory to advance to the AFC title game against the New England Patriots.

One game away from the league championship game, the Colts defeated the Patriots, 38–34, in a thriller.

Next stop for the Colts: the Super Bowl.

Their opponents: the Chicago Bears.

Peyton Manning throws a pass in the second half of Super Bowl XLI at Dolphin Stadium in Miami, Florida, on February 4, 2007. Heavy rain and a slick ball made it more difficult for Manning to throw accurately.

Super Day

Rain came down in buckets. It was Super Bowl XLI and the Colts' players dug in for the biggest game of their lives. For Peyton Manning, that went double.

Now was his chance to finally prove he could win the "big one." Would it rain on Peyton's parade?

The weather report was dire. The day of the game it rained non-stop at Miami's Dolphin Stadium. It would be a real challenge for any quarterback, running back, or receiver to maneuver in such sloppy conditions.

But the poor conditions didn't seem to be a problem once the game started. Chicago's Devin Hester took the opening kickoff and returned it 92 yards for a touchdown. Just like that, the Bears went ahead, 7–0. They had scored in fourteen seconds. It was the first time that anyone had returned the opening kickoff for a touchdown in the Super Bowl.

The Colts were stunned. But not too stunned to recover.

Manning fired a pass to Reggie Wayne, and the wide receiver raced 52 yards for the touchdown. Back came the Bears behind quarterback Rex Grossman to go ahead by eight points.

Trailing 14–6 after one quarter, Manning went to work. First, he moved the Colts into scoring position for Adam Vinatieri's field goal. Then he handed the ball off to Dominic Rhodes, who scored for a 16–14 Indianapolis lead.

More to come. Manning took the Colts on two long drives, each time resulting in field goals.

As the game entered the fourth quarter, the Colts were well on their way to victory. The final score was Indianapolis 29, Chicago 17.

Manning had finally quieted his critics. He had won his first Super Bowl!

"In years past when our team's come up short, it's been disappointing," Manning said. "Somehow we found a way to have learned from some of those losses and we've been a better team because if it."

After falling behind early in the game, Peyton Manning led the Colts on several scoring drives to grab the lead. In this photo, Manning absorbs a hit by Chicago Bears defensive tackle Tank Johnson as he attempts a pass during the first half of the game.

Up Close

Since turning pro in 1998, Manning started every game for the Colts—a total of 227 games through the 2010 season. Unfortunately, his streak ended at the beginning of the 2011 season. Manning could not play during the season because of a neck injury.

On top of the sweet victory, Manning added another trophy to his collection when he was named the game's Most Valuable Player.

Always the team player, Manning shared the glory with everyone else.

"We won as a team," he said. "Everyone has done their part. I am so proud of my team. We have stuck together and this is such a great feeling."

Returning to postseason play became a habit for the Colts. As did winning trophies for Manning. In the 2009 season, he was awarded his fourth league MVP award. That broke the record for most MVP awards for a single player. He also became only the fourth player in NFL history to pass for 50,000 yards. He was the fastest and youngest to reach that mark.

Peyton Manning hoists the Vince Lombardi Trophy after the Colts defeated the Chicago Bears, 29–17, in Super Bowl XLI. Manning also earned Super Bowl MVP honors.

After a terrific regular season in which the Colts started 14–0, Peyton Manning made it back to the Super Bowl. In this photo, Manning runs while looking for a receiver to get open during Super Bowl XLIV. The Colts lost the game, 31–17.

In the 2009 season, the Colts won their first 14 games, threatening to become the first NFL team to go undefeated since the 1972 Miami Dolphins. With a 14–0 record, the Colts had clinched a playoff berth. But should they go for a perfect record? The Colts decided it was more important for their players to be healthy for a Super Bowl run. Resting the starters, they lost their last two regular-season games.

The Colts still went into the playoffs with the NFL's best record at 14–2. After playoff wins over the Baltimore Ravens and the New York Jets, the Colts lost to the New Orleans Saints in the Super Bowl, 31–17.

Despite the difficult loss in the Super Bowl, Manning posted another great season in 2010. But then his career hit a major roadblock. Suffering from pain and weakness in his neck and arm, Manning underwent surgery. The injury forced him to miss the entire 2011 season. Without Manning at quarterback, the Colts stumbled to a 2–14 record.

After the season, the Colts had a decision to make. With the first pick in the 2012 draft, the team could start over with a star college quarterback, or keep Manning. Looking toward the future, the Colts decided to cut ties with their thirty-six-year-old franchise quarterback. The team released Manning on March 7, 2012. He became a free agent.

Denver Broncos quarterback Peyton Manning shows off his new jersey with team owner, Pat Bowlen, left, and executive vice president of football operations, John Elway, during a press conference at the team's headquarters in Englewood, Colorado, on March 20, 2012.

Many teams were eager to sign the great Peyton Manning. It was a tough choice for Manning. On March 20, he signed a five-year contract with the Denver Broncos.

Petyon Manning will still wear number 18 every Sunday but for a new team. Can the future Hall-of-Fame quarterback write a new chapter to his storied career?

Career Statistics

| YEAR | TEAM | PASSING | | | | | | | | | | RUSH TD |
		G	Att	Comp	Pct	Yds	Avg	Yrds/G	TD	Int	QB Rating	TD
1998	Indianapolis	16	575	326	56.7	3,739	6.5	233.77	26	28	71.2	0
1999	Indianapolis	16	533	331	62.1	4,135	7.8	258.4	26	15	90.7	2
2000	Indianapolis	16	571	357	62.5	4,413	7.7	275.8	33	15	94.7	1
2001	Indianapolis	16	547	343	62.7	4,131	7.6	258.2	26	23	84.1	4
2002	Indianapolis	16	591	392	66.3	4,200	7.1	262.5	27	19	88.8	2
2003	Indianapolis	16	566	379	67.0	4,267	7.5	266.7	29	10	99.0	0
2004	Indianapolis	16	497	336	67.6	4,557	9.2	284.8	49	10	121.1	0
2005	Indianapolis	16	453	305	67.3	3,747	8.3	234.2	28	10	104.1	0
2006	Indianapolis	16	557	362	65.0	4,397	7.9	274.8	31	9	101.0	4
2007	Indianapolis	16	515	337	65.4	4,040	7.8	252.5	31	14	98.0	3
2008	Indianapolis	16	555	371	66.8	4,002	7.2	250.1	27	12	95.0	1
2009	Indianapolis	16	571	393	68.8	4,500	7.9	281.2	33	16	99.9	0
2010	Indianapolis	16	679	450	66.3	4,700	6.9	293.8	33	17	91.9	0
2011	Indianapolis	0	—	—	—	—	—	—	—	—	—	0
Total		208	7,210	4,682	64.9	54,828	7.6	263.6	399	198	94.9	17

G–Games played
Att.–Attempts
Comp.–Completions

Pct.–Completion Percentage
Yds.–Yards
Avg.–Yards per Completion

Yrds/G–Yards per Game
TD–Touchdowns
QB Rating–Quarterback Rating

Int.–Interceptions
Rush TD–Rushing Touchdowns

Where to Write to Peyton Manning

Mr. Peyton Manning
c/o Denver Broncos
13655 Broncos Parkway
Englewood, CO 80112

Glossary

draft—A selection of players by teams, who take turns choosing the players they want.

free agent—A professional athlete who is not bound by contract and so is eligible to join any team.

freshman—A ninth-grade student in high school or a first-year student in college.

quarterback—He is in charge of the offense. He calls the plays, sometimes with help from the coach. The quarterback can either pass the ball, hand it off to a running back, or keep it and run.

rookie—A player in his first full season in professional sports.

senior—A twelfth-grade student in high school or a fourth-year student in college.

tight end—Usually a big player who catches passes and blocks for runners.

Further Reading

Books

Artell, Mike. *Peyton Manning: Football Superstar*. Mankato, Minn.: Capstone Press, 2012.

Christopher, Matt. *On the Field With Eli and Peyton Manning*. New York: Little, Brown and Company, 2008.

Glaser, Jason. *Peyton Manning*. York, Pa.: Gareth Stevens Publishing, 2011.

Sandler, Michael. *Peyton Manning*. New York: Bearport Publishing, 2012.

Savage, Jeff. *Peyton Manning*. Minneapolis, Minn.: Lerner Publishing Group, 2008.

Internet Addresses

NFL.com: Peyton Manning Player Profile
<http://www.nfl.com/player/peytonmanning/2501863/profile>

The Official Web site of the Denver Broncos
<http://www.denverbroncos.com/>

Peyton Manning's Peyback Foundation
<http://www.peytonmanning.com/>

Index

A

awards, honors
    Most Valuable Player, 8,
      29, 40
    records, breaking, 23,
      25–26, 31–33, 40

B

Baltimore Ravens, 35, 43
Brady, Tom, 8

C

Chicago Bears, 11, 35, 37–40
Citrus Bowl, 22
Colts-Patriots rivalry, 8
Conerly, Charlie, 25–26

D

Denver Broncos, 44
Dungy, Tony, 9, 10, 35

F

Favre, Brett, 33
football. *See also* Indianapolis
    Colts.
    childhood, 13–15
    college, 19–23
    high school, 15–17

G

Gator Bowl, 21
Green Bay Packers, 33
Grossman, Rex, 38

H

Harrison, Marvin, 29
Hester, Devin, 37

I

Indianapolis Colts
    AFC Championship 2007,
      7–11, 35
    drafting of Manning, 23
    Manning Bowl, 35
    Monday Night Football
      2003, 29
    playoffs 1999, 27–29
    release from team, 43
    rookie season, 25–26
    season 2004, 31–34
    season 2009, 43
    Super Bowl XLI, 11, 35,
      37–40
    Super Bowl XLIV, 43
    Wild Card playoff 2006,
      35
Isidore Newman, 15–17

K

Kansas City Chiefs, 35

M

Manning, Archie, 5, 13
Manning, Cooper, 15, 19
Manning, Eli, 15, 35
Manning, Peyton
    childhood, family life,
      13–17

criticism of, 8
overview, 4–5
practice habits, 15, 26–27
statistics, 34
Marino, Dan, 31
Miami Dolphins, 43
Mungro, James, 33

N

New England Patriots,
    7–11, 35
New Orleans Saints, 5,
    13, 43
New York Giants, 26, 35
New York Jets, 43

O

Ohio State, 22

S

San Diego Chargers, 32–33
Stokley, Brandon, 33

T

Tampa Bay Buccaneers, 29
Tennessee Volunteers,
    19–23

V

Vinatieri, Adam, 38
Virginia Tech Hokies, 21

W

Wayne, Reggie, 38